Early Will I Seek HIM

Andrea C. Dexter MSW

Early Will I Seek HIM

Preface

"In all your ways know *and* acknowledge *and* recognize Him,
And He will make your paths straight *and* smooth [removing obstacles that
block your way].

Proverbs 3:6 Amp

TABLE OF CONTENTS

References

About the Author

INTRODUCTION

.... And Those that Seek Me Early Shall find Me Proverbs 8:17

Magnificent things happen in the mornings. At the crack of dawn nature begins to awaken, birds begin to sing, animals begin to move about, even the atmosphere begins to change. Beautiful colors in the sky transitions from dark hues of gray to vibrant oranges to announce the proceeding sun and all its glory. Its beautiful view to behold.

During the spring we celebrate Easter and one of our churches events is Sun Rise service. The idea behind this early Sunday morning service is to mimic the actions of the Mary's being the first to the tomb of Jesus only to find that He was not there. Upon approaching the tomb, they saw the angel had rolled the stone away and were sitting on the stone door of the tomb, the angels informed them no to be afraid, Jesus was no longer there, and they needed to tell the brethren that Jesus has risen. On their way to tell the disciples, they were greeted by Jesus, once they realized who he was, they fell at his feet and worshipped Him. These ladies arrived early to the tomb and were the first to spread the Good News that Jesus has risen Matt. 28:1-10. Again, magnificent things happens in the early mornings.

What is So important about the first part?

One of the most common practices among successful business owners, multimillionaires, CEO's, or any person in a leadership role is awakening early to begin their day. Currently, my alarm clock is not set to sound off in the mornings. Awakening early started for me about two years ago. On night before, I would ask God to be awakened early on the next day so that I could pray, read, or research and write down any revelations concerning the first book God gave me to write. And like clockwork God would open my eyes every time to read, write, and then prepare for work.

So, what is so important about the first part, Exodus 13:2 Sanctify (consecrate, set apart) to Me all the firstborn [males]; whatever is first to open the womb among the Israelites, both of man and of beast, is Mine (amp). There is distinctive clarity of Gods perspective of the first - Set it apart because it is His. The term first is interpreted as foremost in position, rank, or importance, coming before all others in time or order. The concept of first or beginning, or early, as being acceptable is shown throughout the bible as the way to reverence God with your resources, making life decisions, and in every aspect of life. In this book you will consider the benefits and blessings of Seeking God in the first parts of planning.

Chapter One

Early Will I Seek Him in the Day

I love them that love me; and those that seek me early shall find

me. Proverbs 8:17

Top of the morning to You! This antiquated phrase is an Irish greeting which simply means "the best part of the day to you". This principle is introduced in the bible by God in Genesis 3:8 where Adam and Eve heard the voice of God walking through the Garden of Eden in "cool of the day". Initially after reading the scripture, I assumed that the "cool of the day" meant that God spoke with Adam and Eve in the mornings, but after reviewing several versions of this text, and several commentaries for a clearer understanding, I was informed that the "cool of the day" means in the breeze of the day, or the wind of the afternoon. So, God came looking for Adam and Eve in the winds of the afternoon expecting to commune with them but because of sin, they hide themselves, they were not in the place or time of communion.

Let us conceptualize your personal "cool of the day", the time when you and the Holy Spirit meet and commune. For me, my cool of the day is in the mornings, between the hours of 2 to 5 am. During these times, my environment is still and quiet, but I can hear Him the clearest during these times in the morning. When is your "cool of the day" with God? What is the best part of your day?

In the Beginning...God

Before any tree, before any animal, or any human, there is God. God first in order and rank to outline and provide structure to the remainder. God in the beginning of Genesis looked throughout the Earth and saw that it lacked strategy, it lacked order, it lacked form, it simply lacked. Then God begins to compartmentalize time, then space, then resources Genesis 1:1-12. He spoke order to command the darkness to end and the day to begin. God's authority to command the atmosphere is given to every one of his children. Therefore, morning prayer is vitally important. By seeking and speaking with God early, when the day is without form and void, we have the authority to command order, declare Peace over the day, we can decree there be productivity, let there be safety, or whatever the Holy spirit whispers to you in your prayer time, we have the power through the Holy Spirit to say, "Let there Be" and it will be so.

Seeking God early is a sacrifice. I do not know about everyone else, but I enjoy sleep, especially after a long, stressful day. I thank God daily for allowing us to rest confidently in our beds, while he encamps his angles of protection around us. So, when I am awakened around 2:45 am, I know that God wants to commune. I must be honest; I do not always want to get up and sometimes I do not get up at all. But when I do get up and commune, there is a peace that falls over my day, I can better focus, and it feels as if the anxiousness of the day is subsided all because I spent time with God early in the morning and was able to command order to the rest of the day.

The Watches of the Day and Night

When God wants to talk to me or He wants me to pray for other people or situations, its usually between 2- 5 am in the mornings, if He needs to show me something, He will have me read the Word, pray, then fall back asleep to give me a dream as a warning of things to come. I wondered about this specific time frame of 2 am through 5 am in the mornings. The biblical definition of the word watch is A division of the night. The night was originally divided into three watches (Judges 7:19), but later into four, as we find in the New Testament (Matthew 14:25; Mark 6:48)[1]. According to Webster Dictionary, the word watch is interpreted as the act of keeping awake to guard, protect, or attend, a state of alert and continuous attention, or a watchman or body of watchmen formerly assigned to patrol the streets of a town at night, announce the hours, and act as police.[2] Each watch has a specific focus for spiritual activity and areas of prayer. The **First (Evening) Watch** from 6:00 p.m. – 9:00

p.m. which is a time of quiet reflection. Jesus used the evening watch to go aside and pray. (Matt. 14: 23). **The Second Watch** is from 9:00 p.m. to midnight. This watch is a time when God deals with the enemies that are trying to keep us from entering His perfect plan for our lives. In the natural, this time is characterized by deep darkness (Exodus 12:29-30). It is important for intercessors at this watch to give thanks for the protection of the shadow of God's wing and pray for a visitation from the Lord (Psalms 119:62). **The Third Watch** from midnight to 3:00 a.m. is a period of much spiritual activity. It was the hour that caught Peter denying his Lord, this was also the hour when Paul and Silas were released from prison (Acts 16:25). Often, we are awakened during this time with dreams God has given to us. God uses dreams and visions to bring instruction and counsel to us as we sleep and reveals areas where we need to concentrate our prayers and intercession (Job 33:15-18NIV). **The Fourth Watch** is the morning watch from 3:00 a.m. to 6:00 a.m. The spirit realm takes every word uttered from man as a command and mandate. During this watch God fights for and delivers his people (Exodus 14:24-25). Consecrate all the work for the day and pray for protection for God's people throughout the day. "You will make your prayer to Him, He will hear you, and you will pay your vows. You will also declare a thing and it will be established for you: so that light will shine on your ways." (Job 22:27-28). The early morning **Fifth Watch** is from 6am – 9am. To watch is to set yourself to see what God will say to you. (Hab. 2:1). The practice of waiting to hear the voice of God is essential to all the watches. The daytime watch is the **Sixth Watch** from 9:00 a.m. to noon. It is generally accepted that this time marked both Christ's sentencing by Pilate and crucifixion, and the descent of the Holy Spirit at Pentecost. The Israelites also observed this period as a time for corporate prayer. It was at this daily time of prayer and instruction at the temple that Peter and John were attending when they healed the lame man at the Gate Beautiful (Acts 2: 1-8). **The Seventh Watch** from noon to 3:00 p.m. at mid-day gives an hour of rest and a time to seek the Lord. It was during this watch that Daniel always went home to pray and consequently was thrown into a den of lions. Daniel was delivered from the lions' den, and Daniel's accusers became the lions' dinner instead (Daniel 6:9). **The Eighth Watch** of the day from 3:00-6:00 p.m. sees the close of the business day. The Hour of Power and Triumphant Glory, Time to Remove anything that is limiting. This time is an hour of Revelation, hour of Grace, hour of the voice of the Lord, hour of Triumph. This is the time to die to the world and to self. This was the time God changed history because this watch happens to be the time that Jesus died on the Cross (Matthew 27:45-46 ESV). [1]

Whenever the Holy Spirit gives you an unction, pray according to what he gives topics He drops in your spirit because we do not know how to pray but the Holy spirit himself intercedes for us Romans 8:6.

Chapter Challenge

In Psalms 5:1-3, David seeks God early in the morning and believes God will hear his pleas and David expectantly waits for God answers. Ask God to awaken you early for next three mornings for prayer.

Compare and consider the outcomes of the days when you prayed early in the morning- to other days when you did not. Did you find any differences? Was your day better or worse. Did you feel a sense of peace of God's presence with you all day long? Consider these things.

Chapter Two

Early Will I seek Him in Life....

Train up a child in the way he should go and when he is old, he will not depart from it. Proverbs 22:6

As I grow older, I realize is that it takes a little more time to recall certain information, and I should have taken my Christian walk more seriously in my youth. I went to church, but it was because mama said go, but to say that I fully absorbed the Word of God or even fully embraced the service of God would not be true. I see anointed preacher and teachers of the Gospel and hear how old they were when they accepted the call on their lives at 12 and 13 years old and see how advanced they are in the understanding of God's word and the revelation of the word God has given them and realize they had to have spent a lot of their time seeking God in their more youthful years. The Bible says to train up a child in the way he should go (teaching him to seek God's wisdom and will for his abilities and talents), Even when his is old he will not depart from it Proverbs 22:6. As a child, I was not a writer, but I saw my mother write encouraging letters to family members that were incarcerated and I saw how she served others, especially the elderly women at our church. There was an elderly member of our church that served in many positions until she could no longer do so because of her age and poor sight. My mother would go to her home before service to help her get dressed, bring her to church, take her back home, prepare her dinner and then go to her home to prepare dinner for our home. My Mother did this while being a young mother of three young children and a wife. This may seem like a lot, but I believe this was God's way of using her to train up her children in the way they should go - honoring God by serving people who are in need. Pure and unblemished religion in the sight of God the Father is to visit and look after the fatherless, the widows in their distress and to keep oneself uncontaminated by the world *James* 1:27. Since then, I have seen my mother care for other elderly ladies in the neighborhood and church community. And she would make an extra effort to be kind to a person that society would normally reject. Seeing her serve in this capacity may be one of the reasons why the helping profession is the area that is attractive to me and God called me to serve in this capacity as well. I am currently a licensed social worker and the population I currently work with is the elderly and disabled, my siblings serves or have served the population of the low income, elderly and disabled in some capacity. If we had not witnessed our mother serving in the gift of Helps, we would lack a visual model and understanding of how the Christian walk would include the love of Christ that provokes compassion and service.

Training up a child in the way they should go begins with the parent's relationship with God and their obedience to God. Moses commanded the children of Israel to listen and commit the Word to their hearts, and minds and to teach it to their children- You shall teach the command diligently to your children (impressing God's precepts on their minds and penetrating their hearts with his truths) and shall speak of them when you sit in your house and when you walk on the road, when you lie down and when you get up Deuteronomy 6:6-8 amp. By continually placing God's word as **THE STANDARD** for life before children; a parent is training them up in the way that he should go, and when he is old, he will not depart from it.

Children begin to develop language skills as early as birth to five years of age and the language is better developed in an environment that is rich with sound, sight, and constant, consistent exposure to the speech and sound of others, most children grammatical and linguistic skill mature at 12 years of age [2]. God created the young mind with the capacity to absorb information through consistent audio-visual learning. Therefore, he informs Moses to tell his people to consistently expose the children to the laws of God as seeds sown in the grounds of the young mind to help develop the language of the Word, to cultivate the speech of the Word and develop the application of the Word in their lives and it will continue to produce and reproduce until they are old.

Can a Young Person live a Devoted life as a Christian?

Psalms119:8-10

David has the same question and the answer in Psalms 119:8-10, the answer is Yes, yes, they can by keeping God's word and seeking the Lord with their (our) whole heart. The bible shows several examples of young people who made up their minds to be a servant of God and He used their lives to show his power in the earth. God used the virgin Mary, as an honorable favored vessel to birth His son, our Lord and Savior Jesus Christ. Mary at the time of the birth of Jesus was about 14-16 years old. Wow, what a major responsibility bestowed on a teenager! But the bible says that Mary was chosen from among many women Luke 1:28. Mary was a virgin at the time of immaculate conceptions- meaning when the Holy spirit came upon her to impregnate (saturate, soak, steep) her with Jesus, she had never been with a man physically in a sexual manner ever Luke 1:35. Sounds unfathomable doesn't it? Yes, but this is where Mary's faith becomes prevalent. Even though what she was told by the angel Gabriel would be seen as preposterous by others like the priest Zachariah seen in the previous verses of Luke, Mary immediately believes and responds to Gabriel " I am willing to be used by the Lord, Let it happen to me as you have said" Like 1:38. All it takes is a willing vessel and a mind that is determined to live entirely for God in every area, regardless of the environment around him/her. How can a young man stay on the path of purity? By living according to God's word.

Let us view Daniel's life.

God uses youth to change the minds of nations, God used young people to make idol worshippers realize that their God is the true and living God and were delivered in their trials because of their unwavering faith in God. In the book of Daniel, the king of Judah was overthrown by the King of Babylon, God allowed the besieging of

Judah because Judah's king had done evil in the eyesight of God. When God allows Nebuchadnezzar the Babylon king, to overthrow the Judean king Jehoiakim, Nebuchadnezzar commands his chief official to obtains the spoils from the Saul's temple which included sacred items to be placed in the temples of Babylon idols. Along with the gold and other precious items, King Nebuchadnezzar wanted to take some of the choice children to serve in his kingdom, these children had to be the crème de la crème, the best of the best children to serve him. These children were knowledgeable, skillful, comprehensive learners, and looked good. Among the children that were taken from Judah were four young men named, Daniel, Hananiah, Mishael, and Azariah. These young men were around the age of fourteen to sixteen years of age when they were removed from their homeland. Even though these young men where away from their families, they wanted to remain loyal to God and the faith that they were taught in their homelands. Daniel decides to make an outward example of his devotion to God by not defiling himself by eating the Kings food. Daniel also influences the other young men that were taken captive with him to do likewise, not eat the Kings food. Let me clarify, eating food does not make you better or worse in Gods eyes, but taking in the ways of this world in a temple that is sanctified for God's use is sin, so Daniels's demeanor was to show outwardly what his conviction was in his spirit- to remain pure and undefiled. Because of the young men's determination not to defile themselves with ways of the Babylonian country, God honored their sacrifice and granted them knowledge and skill in all areas of learning and wisdom. God also made them to be found better than the other Chaldeans, and in addition to this God gave Daniel a special skill that no other native from Babylon possessed *Daniel 1:1-21*.

God used the lives of those young men to show his power by the trials that the king of that world placed on them because they decided not to bow and worship idols.

God uses the giftings of the Young person.

God gives each one of us something we can use for his Glory, He gives it to us in our youth, but the gift must be cultivated in an environment so that it can be used and produce fruits. Daniels's gift was deciphering dreams, administration, and visions. Daniel may have had this gift before but was not in the area where God can use the gift, display the gifts, and receive glory for the giftings he gave Daniel. God gave the king of Babylon a dream that none of the Babylonian sorcerers, astrologers, or magicians could not interpret. Daniel heard of this, he gathered his friends and encouraged them to pray to God for Daniel to receive an interpretation of the kings' dream. God gave Daniel the interpretation of the dream and he explained the dream to King Nebuchadnezzar. The king bowed to worship Daniel, commanded an offering be made unto Daniels in honor of his God, and promoted ruler over the providence of Babylon, and Chief governor over all the Babylonian wise men, and there is more, at Daniels request he appoints Hananiah, Azariah, and Mishaal to handle the affairs of Babylon *Daniel 2:1-49.*

Seeking God early in life not only allows God to use your life to influence your peers, but it also allows God to develop your gifts that will be used to turn the hearts of many people of different nations to God, and God will create opportunities to place you before great men because of the giftings He gave you.

God displays His power in the lives of Hananiah, Mishael and Azariah.

While these young men were living in Babylon, King Nebuchadnezzar had a great golden image, highly erected of himself, and he commanded that all the people, at the sound of music are to fall and worship the image (idol worship). Whoever does not worship the image would be thrown into the fiery furnace (Daniel 3:1-6). The king was informed of Hananiah, Mishael, and Azariah, the appointed supervisors over Babylon, were not bowing at the sound of music to his golden image. Once Nebuchadnezzar heard this, he asked the young men about their decision not to bow and the responded they will not bow nor lower their standard to idol worship Daniel 3:8-17. The king gave them another chance to change their minds and bow in idol worship and being confident in their faith, they told the king that even if God does not rescue us from the fiery furnace, he is more than able to do so. Look at their faith on display. Can God put you in a fiery situation and you will fully trust him amid a trial? Of Course, the king was upset at these young men defying his authority and tell his guards to turn the furnace up seven time hotter, tie the men up and throw them into the furnace. Once the young men were in the furnace, the fire was so hot, that it killed the guards that threw them in, and burned the ropes Hananiah, Mishael, and Azariah were tied in. Not only did the king see the three young men in the furnace, but he also saw one more that looked like the son of God Daniel 3:18-24. Once these men were delivered from the furnace the king said blessed be the God of Shadrach, Meshach, and Abednego and created a decree that every people, nation, and language, which speak anything amiss against the God of Shadrach, Meshach, and Abednego, shall be cut in pieces, and their houses shall be made a dunghill: because there is no other God that can deliver after this sort of trial *Daniel 3:29*.

God uses the lives of these young people to change the minds of a nation to turn to God, to influence their culture, and as a result spreading the knowledge the one and only true and Living God. In conclusion… How can a young man stay on the path of purity? By living according to God's word. God can use your life to change a nation.

Take away points from this section:

1. Children's acknowledgment, service to, and reverence of God's word is contingent upon the parents (guardians) exposing them to word by hearing and seeing it applied in their lives.

2. God uses young men and women to influence nations and directs minds to God.

3. God will be with you in the middle of trials because He is well capable.

4. Seek God early in Life for direction because He knows that path which you shall take.

Chapter Three

Early will I seek Him in Relationship

I am a jealous God ... No other Gods before ME. Exodus 20:5-6

Misappropriated relationship

Recently I learned that I have been using other relationships in the placed of my relationship with God. I love my family, I mean love them dearly, but on this week, God revealed to me that my motivation for loving them to the degree that I do is not all genuine. God revealed to me the truth about my admiration for my family, partly I was using them to fill a void only GOD could. And the more time I spent with them, the more I chose them as a distraction for me to keep me from spending that time with God and working on the visions he gave me and exploring the hinderances that keep me in certain bondages and working on goals. So, when the Lord revealed to me the imbalance in the relationship with my family, I had to repent and admit that I was in idol worship.

Idol worship can be anything that is a wrongly appropriated relationship with any person, place, or thing that takes your focus off spending quality time with God. Some examples of idol worship can be working on your appearance to the world, spending more time doing busy work in the building of the church rather than spending time with God, food, drink, shopping, working, obtaining money, becoming popular, etc. All these things can take focus off God if you allow it to. Even dating can be idol worship yes, dating. I remember in my twenties, I kept choosing worldly relationships rather than relationship with God. No matter how hard I tried, it did not work. I can recall one on again and off again relationship with this guy in college. I proclaimed I knew Christ and had accepted HIM as Lord and savior but every so often we would fornicate. I would feel so guilty (after the fact) and repent, and fornicate again, repent, and repeat. I repeated that cycle of sin and repenting for years. One night during our Spring revival I heard the Lord say clearly "I cannot bless you if you continue what you are doing". I had to repent and tell that person the truth- I cannot continue to so this- Godly grief brings about repentance 2 Cor. 7:10. Well naturally that word from God broke the cycle of idol worship and started me on the path of real authentic relationship. A relationship where I can tell the truth and still be loved. What is authentic? The term means true, truth, lawful, or legitimate or in accordance with the law. For us to have an authentic relationship with God it must be in accordance with his law…No other Gods before me. Because how can a Temple of God have relationship with idols? 2Cor. 6:16

Authentic Relationship with God.

While I was wasting time, spinning my wheels in the cycle of sin and repentance, dealing in relationships that where not God ordained, God was giving me a chance every day to come into a real authentic relationship with Him by giving me another day to repent. While I was acting as a sinner, He was showing me his love daily with brand new mercies. All the while proclaiming to be a Christian, I was not placing my relationship with God at the forefront of my life. But God was orchestrating the demise of every acquaintanceship I placed before Him- because He is a jealous God. You really do not know how to handle a relationship with others until you have learned relationship with God first. Hebrew meaning of the word relationship is proskollaó which means to glue to, to join. I was choosing to join with people who could not be my source, trying to fill a gap that only God could. I was practicing in idol worship, by giving reverence to a person, holding the relationship in a higher regard than the God of my life by spending time talking until early morning, becoming intimate, being overly concerned with what they were doing, rather than using this same determination in connecting and communing with God. I had to repent.

In the Bible we can see the children of Israel, Gods chosen people had the same issue with cyclic sin and idolatry. God is so serious about idol worship, that he gives the topic top priority to forbid and admonish the act. Exodus 20:3 Do not have other gods besides ME. Exodus 20:4 You shall not make for yourself an image in the form of anything in heaven above or on the earth beneath or in the waters below. God gave these commandments to Moses after he guided the Israelites out of Egypt. The Israelites where actively practicing idol worship while they were in Egypt Joshua 24:14, and because they had been exposed to pagan gods and idol worship for so many years, that when times became challenging for them on their way to the Promised Land, they began to turn to the actions they had become accustomed to such as complaining, not trusting God and later idol worship.

They would believe God and then turn to idol worship- God would punish them they would repent- God would accept them back and forgive them and the cycle would repeat itself. What would make the Israelites continue in the cyclic sins? the exact same thing that blocks the authenticity of our relationship with God- they had become too comfortable with the Almighty God. They became laxed in keeping His commandments and went back into the bondage of sin. To operate in Sin and come to wanting a relationship is an insult to the Highest God. The only way to re-establish a relationship with God is to repent- and turn from the wicked ways. One of the examples my mother would use while teaching Sunday School is that when a person wants to get off drugs or if a person were in AA meeting, the first thing they would have to do is admit they have a problem, and this is the same when it comes to relationship with God, we must be honest, we must admit to God we are sinners and we have sinned. He already knows but God cannot heal what we will not reveal. If we confess our sins, he is faithful and just and will forgive us our sins and purify us from all unrighteousness John 1:9.

Take away from this section:

1. Any relationship placed before God is considered idol worship.

2. Connection and Communion with God fills all internal and relationship voids.

3. When we fall short, God is faithful to forgive, if we confess our sins.

4. You do not know relationship with others until you learn relationship with God first.

5. God cannot heal what we do not reveal.

Chapter Four

Early Will I Seek Him ...In Prayer

So, I say unto you, keep asking, and it will be given to you. Keep searching and you will find. Keep knocking and the door will be opened to you. Luke 11:9

In September 2014, after years of being a renter, the Lord allowed me to become a homeowner. In the years of No's, the Lord allowed a Yes concerning me and purchasing a home. Once we moved into the new community, I found that some young children lived down that street liked to knock on neighbors' doors and take off running. Because of the children's continual playing at the neighbors' homes, the kids eventually got reprimanded and the knocking stopped.

In Luke 11 Jesus is praying and one of his disciples sees him and asks Him to teach them how to pray. Jesus begins to teach then and gives his disciples the structure of prayer, we refer to this as the Lord's prayer. Jesus has a way to give examples of what the scripture is saying called parables to ensure that the disciples fully understood the message in the teachings. Jesus begin to teach the disciples the parable in Luke 11. He said suppose you go to your friend's house at midnight and ask him to borrow 3 loaves of bread because you are having guest over and you have nothing to offer them. But the friend responds, look its late, my family and I are in bed and the door is locked so "Don't bother me". Jesus tells his disciples that it is not the fact that his friends is at the door that makes the man get out of bed and open the door, it is the shameless, persistent, continual knocking at the door of his home that makes him act. This is what God wants us to do, pray without ceasing- I Thessalonians 5:17. It is not that God does not hear us the first time we pray. It is not because we do not trust God by praying over and over, time and time again. God wants continual cultivation of our relationship with Him and constant dependency on Him. Continuing prayer gives us the opportunity to talk to God about our concerns, cast our issues of life at his feet, and pray on the behalf of others. Our persistent prayers does not change God's will it changes our will. For example, Jesus in the Garden of Gethsemane prayed "if it be possible let this cup pass nevertheless not as I will, but as thou wilt". Matt 26:39 kjv. Jesus asks if it is possible to negate this task of being beaten, and hung on the cross for our sins, but the prayer ends with what is more important to Him- completing the will of God. Personally, I recognize that our human will is selfish, vainglorious, and self-seeking. But when you walk in Gods will for your life this is seeking first the Kingdom, and until our will matches Gods, our prayers will not be answered. Your will be done on earth as it is in heaven Luke 11:2. Therefore Jesus gives us the model in Luke 11:1-5 and Matt. 6:13. There is no vain glory or ill will listed in this prayer, but rather the model prayer showed honor and reverence of God as being our father, the one who knows best for us and we desire his will over our own. We want the environment on Earth to operate as the Kingdom in Heaven. For us to pray that Gods Kingdom come, we must first know what Gods Kingdom is.

The Kingdom of Heaven is like....

The parables in Matthew 13: 1-53. Jesus gives several examples of the Kingdom of Heaven. He stated that Kingdom of heaven is like seed to the sower, available to everyone but some will not accept. The kingdom of heaven is like wheat and weeds growing together, looking just alike but one has no value and will be destroyed when the harvester come to separate. The kingdom of heaven is like the mustard seed introduced as small but when the seed has fully matured, as a tree it stands strong in authority, noticeable and can be rested in. Jesus also says that the kingdom of heaven is like valuable treasure and pearls that one must give up everything to obtain. And lastly the Kingdom of Heaven is like a fisherman that casts a large net into the sea and drags it to shore masses of fish only to separate the good catch from the poor fish and throw away the poor ones. I understand the Kingdom of Heaven like this... the opportunity to accept Jesus Christ as our Lord and savior is available for all, one must give up their way of life to obtain valuable treasure of everlasting life. When we choose Christ, the devil tries to steal our confession of faith through trials of life but, it is our choosing to allow satan to take our Confession because he is already a defeated enemy. The Kingdom objectives are growth, expansion, inclusive to all who wants to be a part of the Kingdom, membership cannot be purchased, and one must be willing to live subject to the King.

In the end of time, as the bible states there will be a separation of the True, sold out followers of Christ and the imitators, the ones who just looked the part but did not fully accept the work of Jesus on the cross. The imitations or non-believers will be cast into the fires of hell to burn for an eternity Matt 13:49. The Lord is longsuffering in returning giving us time to repent because it is not his will that any man perish 2 Peter 3:9. For the Kingdom of God is not eating and drinking but righteousness, peace, and joy in the Holy Spirit. Romans 14:17

Pardon in Prayer…

It strikes me odd that in Luke 11:1-5 and in Matthew 6:9-13 both writers give the Lord Prayer verbatim, they have the same account but the following verses Matthew 6:14 and Luke 11:9 goes in the opposite directions. Luke 11:9 says to keep on asking and Matthew says if you do not want to forgive peoples trespasses, God will not forgive your trespasses against him. One scripture says persistence gets prayers answered, and the other scripture says holding unforgiveness keeps us from getting our prayers answered.

The term unforgiving is defined as the unwillingness to forgive or making no allowances for error or weakness. When we pray with an unforgiving heart or while holding onto offense, we are technically wasting our time. When we hold grudges and unforgiveness in our hearts we are operating under the conceptualization of we would like God to allow us no room for error nor weakness just as We have no allowances for our fellow man (woman). I really do not want to fall in the hands of an unforgiving God. And neither do you. God promises us in His word that if we hold unforgiveness in our hearts, He will not forgive our sins Mark 11:25 nor accepts our worship Matthew 5:23-24.

Posture in Prayer

I know one of the roots of unforgiveness is pride. The biblical definition of pride is high, arrogant, placing oneself higher that God, placing confidence in self not God. Now, how can an exalted one pray to THE Exalted One? They cannot. Most often when I am offended or when I talk about being offended – one can notice the undertone of the conversation sound like "How can you do this to ME?" Not ME! I am ME! You see how that sounds the exalt of self, the flesh, pride. That flesh must be killed daily if not it will try to stand before God and no pride can stand before GOD. James 4:6 God resist the proud but gives grace to the humble.

Question, would you rather hold on to something that has lesser or no value at all? Well holding onto unforgiveness is like keep the valueless thing rather than opening your hands to the blessing of communication with the Father- a gift of more value. Unforgiveness only hinders your prayers and allows for the reaping of unforgiveness for the offenses you have sown toward The Father.

The opposite of pride is humility. Humility is defined as the freedom from pride and arrogance, humbleness of mind and modest estimate of one's own self-worth. In prayer we must approach the God in humility. Even though Jesus, who was a part of the Triune God head, who existed on Earth as Word made flesh, was humble. Jesus humbles himself by assuming the form of a slave, HE humbles himself by becoming obedient, even unto the point of death on the cross. Philippians 2:6-8. For us to approach God in prayer we must have approached God in the humbleness of obedience. God had commanded us to forgive- a task that is not unattainable for the Christian. God never commanded us to do something that we do not have the ability to accomplish with His help of course, For we can do all things with the help of the Lord.

Matthew 18:4 Therefore whoever humbles himself like this child- this one is the greatest in the Kingdom of Heaven. Kids already know that they have limitations in height, size, and in knowledge. That is why children ask so many questions to their parents or guardians. They recognizes their limits and ask with confidence with the mindset of My Father can give me what I want or need. In prayer we must approach God with this same childlike humility, acknowledging God our father is all powerful, all knowing, understanding that we are limited but HE is everlasting and is well capable to do what we are requesting.

Prerequisite of Prayer.

When reading and writing this text God kept giving me words that started with the letter P as a characteristic of prayer. There is a prerequisite of prayer to having prayers heard. The term prerequisite is defined as something requires as a prior condition for something else to happen or exist. In 2 Chronicles 7, King Solomon was finished building the Temple for the Lord, he was ending the prayer of dedication to the Lord, when the Lord sent a fire down to the altar consuming all the burnt offerings and God Glory filled the temple. Later the Lord appeared to Solomon in a dream and told Him God heard his prayers and have chosen this place as temple of sacrifice. God also told Solomon that if HE chooses to close the sky and stop the rains or send grasshoppers to consume the land and pestilence His people, with prior criteria met, can pray, and ask him to stop. God gives the prerequisite to answered prayers in 2Chronicles 7:14. If my people, which are called by my name, shall humble themselves, and pray, and seek my face, and turn from their wicked ways; then will I hear from heaven, and will forgive their sin, and will heal their land. Let us break down the prerequisite down.

If my people who are called by my name…

Growing up I have a nickname I think my uncles gave it to me as a child, but now as an adult I know how you know me by the name you call me. If you call me by my childhood nickname, I know that you probably know me from my hometown, where we probably went to school or church together, but if you call me by biological birth name, we probably meet in college or work and our relationship have limits. The name entails relationship. In II Chronicles 7:14 the people who are called by God's name has the relationship with HIM. It is the relationship that gives access to God. When the believer prays, we pray in Jesus' name because we have accepted Jesus as the Lord and savior of our lives, AND Jesus is the Way to the Father. God hears the prayers because it bears the name of his Son Jesus, so it is as if the request is coming from his Son. Some people believe that anyone can pray, whether they have accepted Christ or not and they can, but it will not be effectual. Only the believer can have effectual prayers to the Father. It is the prayers of the Righteous that availeth much or have much value James 5:16. The prerequisite for effective prayer is relationship.

Shall Humble themselves and pray….

It is pride in the human nature that prevents us from asking, whether it be for directions, how to fix something, etc, and I am guilty of this too. I would rather do it myself that to ask someone to do it for me or even to help me. Even though this is human nature as believers we are a spiritual being, we are not under our own government. We have a Father that can do any and everything we ask if its according to his will. It is pride that prevents us from asking for help even if the help is from the Creator of the Heavens and Earth. Therefore, God tells Solomon if my people, which are called by my name shall humble themselves and pray, because God knows his people still have the genetic makeup of Adam and Eve wanting to make for themselves a covering and handle situations in their own power, rather than allowing Almighty God to cover them. Prayer should be the very first thing we do when troubles arise not the alternative. Prayer is the communication between man and God, and Humble is the heart posture we must have when communicating with God.

...Seek My Face and turn from their evil ways...

In the verses preceding II Chronicles 7:12-13, God lets Solomon know that his prayers were heard, and He has chosen this place as a temple of Sacrifice. And God further gives Solomon a premise and a promise. If I close the heavens so no rains fall, or if I command the grasshopper to consume the land, or if I send pestilence on My people…. Now wait, why would God send pestilence, grasshoppers, and a drought to His people? Because of Sin. God would use droughts to starve the cattle, grasshoppers to demolish the crops and pestilence to kill His people, to admonish sin. But there is a promise in verse 14, if my people who are called by my name, will humble themselves, pray and seek my face, and turn from their evil ways. In other words, if my people who has sinned against Me will humble down, seek ME, and pray and repent then, we can talk, then I will be able to send an answer to your prayers.

The word repentance is defined as to turn from sin and dedicate oneself to the amendment of one's life. The Greek word for repentance is metanoia which means the change of heart or change of mind. The root of sin is not what is manifested in outward behaviors, no sins root in the heart, and out behavior is the demonstration of what going on in the heart. When we repent, there must be a sincere desire to have the heart and mind to turn away from sin and look to God. From this place of repentance God hears and see the turned heart and mind, this posture catches His attention and God grants the repented favor- Blessed are they that morn for they shall be comforted. Matthew 5:4.

.... Then I will hear from heaven, forgive their sins, and then heal their land.

The Greek word for hear is akouo which means be endowed with the faculty of hearing, not deaf, to attend to, consider what is or has been said. From this Greek word we get the term acoustics- meaning the properties or qualities of a room or building that determine how sound is transmitted in it. Notice how acoustics work- it is usually a sound that is made from a smaller instrument that is amplified without electrical amplification like a speaker. But when sin is present, the unrepented prayer sound has no amplification, it does not reach, and fill a space. God cannot hear the sinner pray unless it is the prayers of repentance. Sin prevent the very ears of God from hearing. Sin stops God hands from moving or even considering moving on his people's behalf. Once God's people repent, the relationship is restored, the line of communication is opened again. Then God can hear through a cleared conduit to send answers to prayers to His people. There will be no hinders in the transmissions of sound from a small instrument to a larger space or in other words from God's people to heavens and from heaven to God people. God says in I Chronicles 7:15 My eyes will now be open, and my ears will be attentive to prayer from this place. God can see us and hear us when we are in a place of repentance and relationship.

Place of prayer

I would usually pray when I first wake in the morning, or while preparing for work in the morning. Thanking God for keeping us through the night without hurt harm or danger, for allowing us to rest in the knowledge of His power, and I thank Him for waking me up with the use of my limbs and fully functioning organ systems, seeing my family, keeping us through tough seasons in life etc. But there is no specific physical location for prayer to take place for me other than in my mind or speaking prayers aloud when my mind becomes too cluttered with thoughts. I often pray while driving going about my daily occupations. The bible tells us to pray without ceasing Luke 18:1.

Often in scripture, we see Jesus praying but he is alone. In Luke 22: 39-41 Jesus leaves the disciples to pray to the Father asking that the "bitter cup" of the cross passes from him before he is betrayed by Judas. In a different account Mark 1:35 gives another occasion Jesus leaves the house early in the morning to go off to a place of solidarity to pray. Also, in Matthew 14:23 After he they blessed and fed the multitude with the fishes and loaves of bread- Jesus send the disciples away, dismisses the crowds and he goes to the mountains alone to pray. Why is he alone praying? In Matthew 6:5 Jesus warns us in against praying to be seen like the hypocrites because they are not really praying to God these people are praying for the show, to be seen, for the fanfare, to hear vainglorious church praises from others or for the promotion of self. The applause from the audience is the hypocrites' reward. But Jesus admonishes us in Matthew 6:6 to go to a secret place, go into your private room, shut your door, and pray to the Father in secret and he will reward you openly. I believe God requires our total attention in prayer because he deserves our honor, and he wants us to be intimate with him in prayer. Do you recall in Genesis 3:8-9 when God walked through the garden in the cool of the day to talk with Adam, before the fall Adam spoke with God without inhibitions? This freedom is available in prayer with the Father. Today's society the social media platform is used to vent about issues, but this is improper behavior to the believers, and in the Catholic church people can confess their sins to a priest, but because we have a High Priest that can be touched with our infirmities and we can tell Him all about it when we go to our secret place and pray. Take care of your soul by telling God everything in prayer.

Power of prayer

Do you recall a commercial for a product that helps to stop a list of aliments (nausea, heartburn upset stomach, diarrhea)? This is how the writer James describes prayer in chapter 5. Prayer is so potent that it is listed as a cure all in James 5:13-18. James wrote that if a person is in trouble, pray. If a person is happy, let them pray in the form of praise. If a person is sick, let them go the elders of the church and let elders anoint them in the name of the Lord and pray. If a person has sinned, confess it, and pray. If you want the environment to change pray like Elijah. Prayer is the answer for everything. But it is not just the talking with God that makes prayer potent, it is the relationship that the man has that makes God act. James 5:16... the effectual fervent prayer of a righteous man availeth much. This means that the passionate persistent prayers of a man in right standing with God is heavy, it has much weight, the prayer has much influence, it will be of effectiveness. God considers them to be precursors for His action and answers. When a righteous man prays it is like adding dynamite to the request- something major is going to take place.

Chapter Challenge

For we do not have a high priest who is unable to empathize with our weaknesses, but we have one who has been tempted in every way, just as we are--yet he did not sin. Hebrews 4:15

Take time to consider that Jesus has been tempted in every way and is able to identify with all human temptations. Do not allow your weaknesses prevent you from praying to the Father. Confess your short comings, sins, and concerns in prayer to the High priest- confess faults one to another God is faithful to forgive.

Chapter Five

Early Will I Seek Him in Thoughts...

...So then with the mind I myself serve the law of God; ...Romans

7:25

The mind is the canvas for creating and learning, the mind can also be the breeding grounds for disillusion and mania. According to its 2019 State of Mental Health in America report:

Over 44 million American adults (18.07%), have a mental health condition. That represents a slight decrease from the 2015 report, which found 18.19% of adults had a mental health condition. The rate of youth experiencing a mental health issue continued rising, and 62% of teens and children with a major depressive episode received no treatment [3].

This statistic is based on the number of individuals that come into a mental health clinic for any type of treatment (medications, counseling, or therapeutic) for any mood disorder such as anxiety, behavioral, emotional disorders. The effects of these mental health diagnosis, if left untreated, can be a hinderance in experiencing a full, productive, and abundant life that has been given to us as a gift through Jesus Christ. The DSM-V definition of mental/ psychiatric disorders is a *behavioral or psychological syndrome or pattern that occurs in an individual b-the consequences of which are clinically significant distress (e.g., a painful symptom) or disability (i.e., impairment in one or more important areas of functioning) ,must not be merely an expectable response to common stressors and losses (for example, the loss of a loved one) or a culturally sanctioned response to an event (for example, trance states in religious rituals), that reflects an underlying psychobiological dysfunction that is not solely a result of social deviance or conflicts with society that has diagnostic validity using one or more sets of diagnostic validators (e.g., prognostic significance, psychobiological disruption, response to treatment) that has clinical utility (for example, contributes to better conceptualization of diagnoses, or to better assessment and treatment)*[4].

I am aware of people can have an imbalance in brain chemistry that causes chronic depression or have experienced traumatic moments in life in which individuals relives through thoughts and individuals can have depressive episodes. For example, in February 2020 the Corona Virus (covid-19) crept into the United States infecting and killing thousands. There was no was no cure, a person did not know they were infected until days after being exposed, and one could be asymptomatic and spread the virus while infected to others. The world

was not prepared to handle this virus that spread like

wildfire nationwide. Businesses shut down, schools closed, social

distancing and isolation caused families, churches, friends to scramble

to find a new normal. Many where overwhelmed with uncertainty, fear,

anxiety, and depression concerning how will I provide for and take care

of my family and myself. During times like these there in an increase

anxious thinking, worrying, depression despair and even suicide. There

are times in my personal life that I have depressive episodes when I

begin to rethink and overthink about the decisions of my past. How I

wish I would have been a better steward of my time or I would have

been better off if I would have taken opportunities more seriously. And

during those moments of thinking (more like regretting) I find myself

not doing something else, not progressing, not being productive or

working on my goals just thinking (regurgitating regret). When the

Lord dropped the Words Will Thou be made whole? In my mind on

my way out the door as I prepared for work, it made me focus on my

thoughts. Everything begins with a thought. In Genesis1:26 there is a

discussion with God the Father, God the son, and God the Holy

Ghost about the blueprint of man before he was created "Let Us

Make". Our thought life is vitally important in serving God, living for God, and accepting the gifts of God.

In John 5 chapter, the scene begins with the arrival of Jesus at the Sheep Gate in Jerusalem after leaving a festival of the Jews. At this gate there was a pool by the name of Bethesda and the name means "House of Mercy". Near this pool there were five colonnades where many people lay who were impotent, blind, halt, withered. Angels came to this pool occasionally to stir the waters of this pool and when this happens, the pool becomes medicinal. Whomever goes into the pool after he stirring the water gets the healing. As Jesus walks through the crowd of Impotent, blind, halt, and withered people, he sees this man and the writer John does not give his name. This man has been at this medicinal pool for 38 years. When Jesus saw him lying there, he knew he had been there for a very long time. Jesus walks to this man, who had been in this spot for a long time, and asks him Will thou be made whole? This man responds "Sir, I have no man, when the waters are troubled, to put me in, because when I am coming, someone goes down ahead of me". John 5:1-7. Let us review- the text did not give the name of the man nor the name of this man illness. I have heard this text preached so many times, but I have never heard it like the Lord dropped in my mind. Maybe this man

was not lame – perhaps he was depressed, and his depression caused

him to lay and be comfortable in the population of people in which he

thought he more closely identified. People who had no vision, people

who had no forward progression, people who were halted

and withdrawn. When this was dropped in my mind, I had to read and

re-read this text in several versions and compare this miracle of healing

to the miracle of healing in Acts 3:6-7 where Apostles Peter and John

looked at lame man refused him monies but commanded him to rise

and walk in the name of Jesus Christ. I also compare

this man's healing in John 5 to another healing in Luke 4:43-48 where

the woman with the issue of blood was healed by touching Jesus in

faith. I then look at the healing of the man with the withered hand in

Mark 3:1-6 where this man's healing is manifested after Jesus examine

the hearts of the Pharisees and commands this man to stretch forth his

hand and his hand was restored. All these miracles of healing shown

me this one thing, Jesus addressed the area in which these people had

an issue. The woman with the issue of blood, the lame man at the gate,

the man with the withered hand, and this man who was there and had

an infirmity thirty-eight years. None of the rest of

these biblical individuals where asked Will thou be made whole, they all had limitations in their physical health, but they were not asked to if they really wanted to be healed. I think Jesus asked this man at the pool of Bethesda, Will thou be made whole, because his illness was not exhibited outside of his own mind. You may be thinking along the same lines as I, the Holy Spirit is intelligent, why didn't Jesus just call that spirit depression, why didn't Jesus ask Will thou be made whole from depression? I had to look at when the word depression was established. The word depression was not an actual word or diagnosis until the 14th century. Jesus looked on this man and saw him lying there he knew he had been there for a long time. How did Jesus know? This man who had been at the Mercy House (Bethesda) was not healed because he had nobody to take him in? When Jesus asks the man Will thou be made whole, he responds Sir I have no man to put me in, when the waters are troubled, while I am coming someone goes down before me. Maybe nobody took him to the pool because they saw that this man was fully capable to move toward the medicinal pool without assistance and but then give up and go back to his comfortable spot beside the pool, close enough to see healing as a bystander, but not enough faith to jump in for his own healing. He may have even said to others when they offered help "I have no man to put me in and while I am coming, someone goes before me" – not realizing help was in front of him.

 After thirty-eight years maybe they (the people who helped others get in the healing pool) saw that to be comfortable in one spot is more important to this man than being healed. Or maybe this man has said to himself for thirty-eight years the one phrase that kept him stuck "I have no man to put me in and while I am coming, someone goes before me." This repetitive, dull, boring, broken record, handicapping phrase "I have no man to put me in and while I am coming, someone goes before me", "I have no man to put me in and while I am coming, someone goes before me", "I have no man to put me in and while I am coming, someone goes before me" … imagine saying this phrase over, and over, and over, and over to yourself, in self talk for thirty-eight years. Like a cow ruminating its food to chew it over again, this man said to himself this phrase over and over. Regurgitating this phrase as if each time he repeats it in his mind, as if it has more justifiable nutrients for him to remain the same.

Let us not judge this man but rather empathize with him. How

many times do we give excuses when we are asked -Will though

be made whole? How many times do we return to the native ways of

thoughts and speech when we are challenged with change? How easy is

it to blame others rather than to take responsibility for our actions?

Back to the scripture, Jesus does not explore this man's answer,

He does not really address his response at all, and He does not take

him to the pool for healing. Jesus tells this man "Rise up, take up your

bed and walk "and immediately he was made whole John 5:9.

Let this mind be in you that is in Christ Jesus.

One on the reasons this man's healing to me is profound is the manner

of thoughts of Jesus has toward this man compared to the manner

of thoughts this man thinks to himself to keep him bound. Imagine

how this text would have been written if this man thought and

repeated to himself, is there anything too hard for God or He is the

great I AM, or God can do the impossible for me. Healthy self-

talk stems from first acknowledging God as the creator of good things.

And He created you and He said it was not only good but

Very Good Gen 1:31.

This day in time it is easy to become bombarded with influences that are negative and to think that if you do not drive this type of vehicle, if your skin is a different color, you may be a specific age or gender or if you do not have a particular income or dress a certain way you can be considered as less than. But this is not the truth, the truth is that we are the best we can be when we are in Christ. We should rehearse in our minds the truth of Gods words. For example, God is our exceeding great reward Gen 15:1. The Lord is our Banner Exodus 17:15; he is our provider Gen 22:14, and it is in Him do we live, move, and have our being Acts 17:28. He is a rewarder of them that diligently seek Him Heb. 11:6, we are Joint heirs to the kingdom, I am the beloved, I am made wonderfully, I am redeemed by the blood of the lamb, I am the apple of his eye, His love for me is everlasting, His faithful love will follow me for a thousand generations. Practice saying these phrases in self talk aloud and this will lift any heavy, depressive feelings of doubt.

Chapter Challenge:

There are many books on mind hacking- how to re-wire your brain in 21 days. Not all are biblical- So I challenge you to use the law of I Am-to change the carnal mind to a mind that immediately produces Christ like thoughts about yourself so that positive experiences are attracted to you. For the next 21 days, each morning get up go to the mirror and say a positive I AM statement to aloud yourself. Below you can see the 21 I Am statements I used. Feel free to use these or search the Bible to find some that are more fitting for you.

I AM: Healed, Loved, Whole, Free, Righteous, an Heiress, His image, Sanctified, Bold, Courageous, Covered, Thankful, Enough, A Believer, Atoned, a Receiver of Mercies, a Lover of his Word, Forgiven, Content, His child.

Chapter Six

Early Will I Seek Him in Covenant...

I will establish MY covenant between me, and you and I will multiply

you greatly. Genesis 17:2

When it comes to covenant relationship, my mind is lead to the book of
Genesis when it speaks of the man without children becoming the father of
many nations. Abram's call by GOD is the one which many can readily
identify with the ebbs and flows of thoughts while waiting for promises of
covenant to be fulfilled.

First let us define covenant in biblical terms. The word covenant is
interpreted as an agreement, a treaty, pact, a deal. Covenant presupposes two
or more parties who come together to make a contract, agreeing on promises,
stipulations, privileges, and responsibilities. The old testament meaning of
covenant is the conditional promises made to humanity by God (the covenant
of works), as revealed in Scripture, the agreement between God and the
ancient Israelites, in which God promised to protect them if they kept His law
and were faithful to Him.

Abrams relational journey begins with God as a senior citizen. God calls
Abram out of his father's homeland to unclear destination. God promises

Abram to make him a father to many nations of people, at this time Abram was 75 years of age and had no children at all. God makes promises to Abram that He will be blessed, Abram's name will be great, and he will be a blessing. Anyone who blesses Abram would be blessed and anyone who tries to curse, or harm Abram would reap the same, and all the people on earth will be blessed through Abram (Gen. 12:2-3).

Covenant relationship requires trust. Abram native homeland was Ur of the Chaldeans, where Terah - Abram father, worshipped idols Joshua 24:2. Abram had to hear and trust a voice that was unlike the other gods he heard his father speak of – to leave and go to an unknown place and to trust God to have children in his older age. Abram had blind faith to follow God to a place he has not seen before and allow God to give him something that was impossible, but is anything too hard for the God of all flesh? Nope, not nothing.

Covenant relations requires sacrifice. As Abram travels at each place, he stops and makes an altar. He stops in Canaan. The Lord tells him he will give this land to his offspring, Abram builds an altar (Gen 12:6-7). Travels further and settles between Bethel and Ai, and Abram pitches a tent and builds an altar to worship God (gen 12:8-9). Covenant relationship includes remembering to acknowledge God in all your ways, in every milestone acknowledge that God is the reason we are here at this point currently.

Abram builds altars to offer sacrifices unto the Lord. Understanding that to receive from God there must be an offering, the giving up of something unto the Lord. Wherever there is an advancement season in life there was something that must be sacrificed whether it be friends, relationships, time, a job, even old offenses- if God requires it for advancement- give it up. But the forward progression was always better for me than remaining in the current situation, and it gets you closer to the promises of God has for you. I remember when I was complaining to God about an offense while cleaning my house, I heard God say very clearly "all that you have needed, Have I Not provided?" Immediately my mind went to I was cleaning my bathroom, in my house, and two years prior I was on the verge of getting evicted from my apartment for late rent. I remembered how I could feel the loan officers condescending looks while applied for home loans and they would tell me I had too much student loan debt, and I remembered when I moved out of my parents' house my sibling and I sold plasma to get gas money to go to work. I honestly had **NO** right to complaint because EVERYTHING I NEEDED GOD HAS SUPPLIED! God statement was an indicator to me that holding on to an old offence was gratuitous, and if God commanded me to release both the offense and the relationship – I no longer needed it. Abraham gives up the relationships and familiarity with his native land for a God in whom he does not really know. Currently, I feel, like many people, the tugging on my spirit man to give up something that I hold dear and near to me. My will, my way in exchange for HIS, it tough but covenant requires sacrifice.

Covenant relationship requires contract. The word of God came to Abram in a vision, telling Abram not to be afraid, because God is his reward. Abram expresses his concern about not having an heir. I admire Abram in this portion of scripture because Abram was beyond the excitement of the prophesy, instead he was concerned about the manifestation of the promise. Have you ever felt the same as Abram, you Heard the prophecy but was ready for the promise to come into fruition? So, we can understand the tone which Abram was speaking to God. Consider this, he moved into an unknown country, away from his people, he was promised to be made into a great nation, and Abram's name would be great. All these promises without the first child. Abram was about 100 years old when Isaac is born. Imagine the doubt starting to creep in his mind at 75 years of age when he obeyed God and moves and 25 years later seeing the heir he was promised being born from a barren wife. Unbelievable right? But God is unlike man, he cannot lie, if He promised it to you, He would do it because He is bound by His word. I believe God saw the concerns turning to doubt in the mind of Abram the CEB version of Gen15:4 says that "the Lords words came Immediately to Abram" assuring him that his heir will not be Eleazar his steward of his house. God confirms His promise to Abram by showing him a visual illustration of how many children he will have by telling Abram to "count the stars" because the number of children that will come from your loins will be innumerable. And Abram believed God without the promise being fulfilled and it was count to him as righteousness.

There is something to be recognized in the times and verses between the tithe given to the priest and the covenant God made with Abram. Examine Genesis 12-15 chapters. Abram was told by the Lord to leave his father's country- Abram obeyed, Abram built altars unto God, God promised Abram his seed would be like the dust, too many to count, Gen 13:16. Then God tells Abram that He is his great reward for his obedience, Abram has questions about blessings for generations and he has no heir? Abram's logic is a generational blessing with no heir??? How can this be? God assures Abram of his promise to him by going into blood covenant or signed a contract in blood with him. God tells Abram to get a heifer 3 years of age, a female goat 3yrs of age, a ram 3 years of age, a turtle dove, and a pigeon and cut them in half. The epitome of this ritual is may we experience the same as these animals if one of us breaks this contract. Abram obeyed God and followed the instruction he was given. Abram waited on God, he drove away the birds of prey, that came to take the sacrifice and still he waited more. (Ok this is a teachable moment.) For anyone who is reading this, allow the word to encourage you, even though we are waiting for God to fulfill the promises, waiting for God to fulfil the prophecy, do not allow the birds of prey to come in and take your expectation for the things God has for you. So, drive out doubt, drive out fear, drive out depression, anything that comes to take focus off the fulfillment of God's word. Abram fell asleep and God walked through the cut animals therefore making himself both persons to complete the contractual covenant. God assures Abram that the promises will be fulfilled because he went into contract with himself- not man. Be reassured that if God promised it to you, he is held by His word. So, drive it OUT the doubt and REST until He fulfills.

Covenant relationship requires Full commitment. God tells Abram HE will establish a covenant with Abram, but there is always a sacrifice, there is always something that must be given to receive. The sacrifice for Abram in 17:10-11 was the foreskin of every male of his offspring to keep the covenant between God and his seed for generations, this happens by the time the male is 8 years of age.

Today's seed of Abraham still must undergo circumcision but not of the foreskin, this circumcision requires the cutting away from the heart. The circumcision of the heart is what is required for the everlasting covenant. God test the heart to see what is more important – the creator or the creations, the blesser or the blessings, the God of flesh or the flesh over god. For example, in Genesis 22:1-19, Abrams final heart check was when God wanted him to sacrifice his promised son Isaac. God tell Abram to make an altar to sacrifice his son to the Lord gave him. Abram does everything God ask him to do, even as to go as far as take his grown son and tie him down to the altar. Abraham was so committed to God that the angel had to call his name twice so that he would stop from killing Isaac. During this quarantine time, God has given us this opportunity to get away from the busyness and do heart checks, to see what we are willing to let go of to keep our covenants intact or receives the promises of the covenant with God. After this test God knew that there is nothing Abraham could not be trusted with because God knew Abraham had given his heart to Him and the stuff (father of many nations) was a bonus benefit of the covenant between God and Abraham. Perhaps many of our test and trials are to check to see where our heart lies, are we fully circumcised, the ways of this world being fully torn from us, or we have limits in our spiritual walk. When it comes to covenant relationship with God where does your heart lie?? Are you fully committed, totally in or not?

Chapter Challenge

God told Abraham to sacrifice the very thing God promised Him- His promised son Isaac. What thing, person, activity would you have trouble in giving up if God requires if to be a sacrifice unto him? In your prayer time

ask God to reveal to you reason behind the attachment(s).

Chapter Seven

Early will I Seek Him in Finances

Will a Man Rob God? Yet ye have robbed me. But you say Where in have we robbed thee. In tithes and offerings. Malachi 3:8-9.

Have you ever heard this phrase? All the church do is ask for money. I have heard it and at one time was guilty of saying it myself. What exactly is the tithe and why can't we just keep all our money? The answer is the tithe is not yours to keep. The word tithe is defined as the tenth part of agriculture, produce, or personal income set apart as an offering to God or for works of mercy, or the same amount regarded as an obligation or tax for the support of the church, priesthood, or the like. Tithing is a biblical principal that honors God and creates room for the blessing on the resources that He allowed us to obtain. Tithing was unofficially introduced to us by Abram in Genesis 14:20. Abram gave the King Melchizedek the tithes of his spoils of war when he and his army defeated the Kings of Elam, Shinar, Ellazar, and Goiium. It is officially written in Mosaic Law where the tenth was a practical acknowledgment of the divine priesthood of Melchizedek, for the tenth was, according to the general custom, the offering presented to Deity. The action of paying tithes is an act of worship- we are giving to Him a portion of the resource he gave us. For example, we use the breath in our body to sing praises and speak well of God this is the same breath he used to bring Adam to life- breath that He gave us the capacity to use. God commands us to give a one-tenth of our resources to the storehouse so that the churches and temples can continue to function. And as an added benefit, of giving the tithe in faith, God even challenges us to prove Him when paying the whole tithe, to see if He will not open the windows of heaven for more blessings and favor. Then God will prevent the evil thing from robbing your harvest (your investments, your efforts of increase) and he will allow for your harvest to be plentiful, so much so that you will be observed by many people because blessing of paying tithes will make you visually prosperous and delightful. People will want to know what you are doing to be so blessed and you can tell them... I am a tither. There are artists in music and film who may not be committed to Christianity but understand the blessing of the tithes. They want to experience the benefits of giving the tithe in their homes and lives. God has blessed these performers careers to endure time, trends, and their influence has lasted and for decades. If you choose not to pay the tithe you are willing deciding to operate under a curse in a fallen world, God has no obligation to bless, cover protect, rebuke devour, or make the areas in which you operate productive and efficient, and you will look like you do not pay the tithe Malachi 3:8-11. The tithes equals covenant.

The concept of paying tithes had become concrete for me when God gave me a dream. In the dream a famous gospel recording artist / preacher and myself were sitting down at a table, having a conversation about paying tithes and the benefits that are available for the tither and generational blessings for the bloodline because of the tither. Through this dream God revealed to me the generational benefits of bringing the meat into His store house would provider for my house for generations. Currently my perspective is that ten percent of your check will not pay off all your debt but paying the tithe to the Lord can get you out of debt.

<u>*Points to remember-*</u>

- Paying your tithes benefits you more than it benefits the preacher.
- God can trust you with more when your heart's will be to do right with resources.
- Paying the tithes give you the opportunity to test God and see if he will not pour you out a blessing.
- The tithe is not yours to withhold from God.

Chapter Eight

Early Will I Seek I Seek Him for Marriage

He that finds a wife Finds a good thing and favor from the Lord.

Proverbs 18:22

The gift of marriage is the covenant that resembles Christ love for the church. Paul writes in Ephesians and compares the wife's submission to the husband to the church submitting itself to Christ. The bible say that the husband is head of the wife, as also Christ is head of the church; and He is the Savior of the body. Therefore, just as the church is subject to Christ, so *let* the wives *be to their **own*** husbands in everything. Ephesians 5:23-24. Marriage is a major decision that can change the trajectory and quality of a person life. The person you plan to marry is a decision that needs to be considered with much prayer, counseling and not just based on a euphoric feeling. God knows more about a person than you do. Since I have gotten older, I do not waste much time when I meet a guy or if a guy shows interest in me, I immediately go to God in prayer and ask HIM "if he is for Me Show me, if he is not for me Show me". Later in a dream, God will show me if the person is stable, not seriously looking for a relationship, or if the guy is sent by Satan only there to be a distraction. I trust Gods answer because HE is all knowing, and I am not. I will encourage you to do the same, on your next interaction, whether it be a potential romantic relationship, friendship, or business relationship ask God this question with sincerity "God, if this is for me Show me, if this is not for me, Show me." When he gives you his answer, accept it- especially if the answer is no, because God sees the entire story where you can only see a snapshot. An attachment to a relationship that is not ordained by God is a waste of time, energy, resources, mental stamina, and can leave you emotionally (and maybe physically) scarred.

Since marriage is a covenant union created by God between a man and a woman in Genesis, we need to ask Him about his creation. The story of Ruth and Boaz found in the book of Ruth, is one that is often used in single conferences, where the widowed Ruth under the advice of her mother-in-law Naomi, was instructed on how to gain the admiration of her future husband Boaz. We single women need to review and obtain the wisdom of Naomi's instruction to Ruth. Ladies we need to listen to the wise counsel of a seasoned women who has remained faithful to her own husband, kept her house Titus (2:3-5). Work and maintain your responsibilities until the man that God has for you is presented. Make yourself available, I mean be available for real, not intertwined with other relationships or friends with benefits, that would prevent you from being available when Boaz comes into the picture. I understand that becoming available is a challenge especially when you have become attached to the wrong person for a long time. But I challenge you to ask God for a strategy on how to untangle this behavior of spending (wasting time) with the wrong person. I can remember when God showed me how to unlearn this behavior of wasting time with the wrong person. He told me to replace that talk time with time in communion with Him learning of Him loving Him. And it works learning of the Lord will heal past hurts from failed relationships and prepare you emotionally for Boaz. Boaz was an established man. He had himself together before marriage. He owned fields, was counseled by elders, a prominent man of noble character and capable to take care of Ruth and Naomi. He had resources to purchases Ruth deceased husbands land to keep his name on it.

Today some women pursue men that have absolutely nothing to offer. The roles are reversed, men instead look to the women to take care of them. My advice ladies, if you considering him for marriage, make sure he can take care of himself and his household before you come along, (even Adam had a job before God gave him Eve). Women make sure you know how to take care of yourselves and manage a household as well. No man wants to marry a burden. We women are nurturers, we are help meets, we manage our homes, we care for our children, we are powerful, beautiful, and resilient, but we do not give birth to grown men. Guys do not marry a Jezebel. A woman with a controlling, self-serving, egotistical, wicked heart, can use these same nurturing traits to become manipulators, predators and seduce, entrap, entangle, and emotionally damage vulnerable people. These women have a very persuasive persistence, that is a deceptive method of control, and use it as a method to break the will of a man, and this not the will of God (men can carry the Jezebel spirit also). Men walk in the authority God gave Adam to have dominion ,be fruitful, multiply, and replenish Gen 1:26-28. Guys seek God for a wife that loves God first – find your wife in Christ- you will find favor from God. King Solomon said Better to live in a desert than with a quarrelsome and nagging wife Proverbs 21:19. I guess the desert would be quieter. Seek God first and choose your mate wisely.

In the bible there are two marriages that God ordained but I would look at as unseemly. Samson and Hosea, two men who God uses their relationships to kill the enemies of God, to execute judgement on the land, and to exhibit Gods faithful love towards his chosen people. Let us begin with Samson.

Samson

The name Samson from its Hebrew origin means sun or sun child. Samson mother was barren, until the Lord sent an angel to tell her that she will have a son Judges 13:3. Samson was ordained as a Nazarite before he was conceived. Samson mother had to become the Nazirite environment that her baby developed in while in her womb. The angel instructed his mother that she was not to drink wine or other alcoholic beverages or eat anything unclean because her son would be set aside for God to use him to save Israel from the power of the Philistines Judges 13:4-5. This is important for parents, when raising children, parents must create the clean, moral environment that is conducive for their children. This will be the example that children see in the home how morals are applied, where they choose to live by example or not when they grow up, at least they are exposed. Samson did not have the liberty of choosing what he wanted to be when he grew up because he was chosen before the beginning of time to be a Nazarite- set aside for God to use. The Nazarites life was one of purity, no strong drink, no eating the unclean things, and he was to let no razor come to his head (no haircuts) Number 6:1-21. Samson was born and grew, and the Lord blessed him. Samson saw a woman that he wanted to marry, she was a Philistine, a group of people who were not in covenant with God. Samsons parents tries to influence him to choose a woman from his own tribe, someone with the same views as himself, because in Deuteronomy 7:2-3 they were commanded by God not to intermarry with the enemies of God because they would turn them away from worshipping God. Samson told his father he wanted the young woman from Timnah for his wife. His parents wanted to talk him out of marrying the woman form Timnah, but God placed the desire for this woman in Samsons heart to later use it as an opportunity to destroy the enemy. We do not always understand why our loved ones choose who they love/ marry, it could be that affinity to this person is God ordained so that He can use their relationship to come against a sinful, prideful, arrogant way of thinking that "my family is too good to marry that person", when God calls Christians to a standard of loving all people, especially those whom others consider unlovable. Samson marries the woman from Timnah and presents the city with a riddle during their wedding celebration. The prize for answering the riddle was 30 sheets of linen and 30 changes of clothes. No one could answer the riddle, so the people pressed his Wife, and she gave them the answer. Samson found out, got upset with the people for pressing his wife for the answer to his riddle and killed 30 men gave the men's clothing and gear that he killed to the person who answered the riddle and went back to his father's home. While Samson was gone, his father-in-law gave his wife to one Samsons friends since he left her after she gave away the answer to his riddle. Samson became so angry and set the Philistines fields of grain on fire, as well as the vineyards, and the olive groves. Samson destroyed their resources and the potential for harvest just like he felt his father-in-law had done to him. Throughout Judges 14-16 chapters, when the Spirit of the Lord came upon Samson, he destroyed the enemies of God. The Philistines wondered where Samsons strength came from but when you have a relationship with God, he can use you to do impossible things. At the end of Samson life, he killed more enemies of God in one day when he took out the pillars in the temple than he did his entire life. Do not allow your sin to prevent you from doing God will and purpose for your life, repent and seek God for help to complete his will. Even though Samson did not do everything according to the Nazarite standards, God still used him, and He is listed in Hebrews 11:32 as a hero of faith.

Hosea

Often, I debate in my mind about being married. I understand how God views covenant and I, at times, do not have the same views. So, when reading about Hosea's call to marry a harlot to show Israel how God will reject and reconcile covenant through repentance leaves me asking, Would I be willing to do this if God called me to marry for an example to his people of his faithful love? Would You? The bible say that believers are not to be yoked with unbelievers (2Cor. 6:14), and as an outsider looking in marriage is work without the added harlotry, but how would you feel knowing that your spouse is outside of the covenant acting like a harlot? Embarrassed, humiliated, heartaches, knowing people are gossiping what will be your demeanor? Our natural tendency is to hold resentment and leave the marriage covenant with that harlot spouse. But for us to remain in a marriage covenant with the harlot spouse means there must be another nature working in us, the nature of Christ. Hosea is a prophet in the Northern Kingdom of Israel around 715-722 B.C., whose obedience to God is upstanding. Hosea chapters 1 -3 is love story if I have ever seen one, God tells the prophet Hosea to marry Gomer, a prostitute, and have children with her. God tells him to name the children Jezreel, Lo-Ruhamah, and Lo-Ammi (God-sows, Not-pitied, and Not-my-people) as examples of how God will judge Israel for the looking to other gods for relationship and provision, when he has supplied all their needs and has delivered them out of the hands of the bondage. God calls Israel promiscuous, and adulterous because they cheated on Him with other gods. And they believed the other gods as their provider. What a slap in the face of God? Hence, God cuts off the provision, sends Israel to a desolate place. In these chapters Gomer is behaving as Israel, going after other men, believing the other men as her provision, until her actions has gotten her sold into slavery. Sin and idolatry does not show the bondage side of itself when it is presented. Sin always takes you to bondage and death (spiritually, physically, or both). If Gomer knew initially that harlotry would have entrapped her do you think she would have willingly become a prostitute? I do not think she would have because it is the casual dedication that is alluring to Gomer/Israel. It is not being totally committed to anything that pulls Gomer/ Israel back into idolatry and bondage. Let us look at currently at ourselves and our covenant with God, are we totally committed in every way? Does the lullaby of the world woo us back and forth between being fully committed and fully backslidden?

Although God cuts Israel off from his provisions to show them that He is their lover, provider, and deliverer, him only. Gods heart still yearns for His chosen people. God tells Hosea to go buy Gomer out of slavery and tell her that no more will you play the harlot, no more will you seek after other gods, you will abide with me for many days, and I will be for you. That is relentless love, a love that will give its all to purchase us from the bondage of sin (sounds familiar).

Oh how, romantic!! We can experience this type of love daily. Every day God gives us this type of unfailing Love, grace, and brand-new mercies. The type of love that looks past our grimy little arrogant, prideful selves and still wants relationship with us……. My God, that is unfailing love.

Points to Remember.

- Marriage covenant is the visible model and example of Christ love for his bride the Church. Husbands need to be submitted under Christ and Wives under husbands, children under parents- every person is under a level of authority.

- God uses marriages to show his relentless, unfailing love, and the union joining a man and woman together in covenant with himself.

- God will restore covenant of relationship contingent on repentance.

- God will set our affections to the one he ordains for our spouse.

Chapter Nine

Early Will I Seek Him to Satisfy my Soul

For I have satiated the weary soul, and I have replenished every sorrowful soul.
Jeremiah 30:25

One of the phrases that my sister and I use is "God plays chess not checkers". It is not biblical but to us it makes sense. It shows how strategic God is when getting His will done. The story of the Samaritan woman at the well in John 4 is one that we can see tactical planning at its best. This woman like many of us was thirsty, but not dehydrated, this thirst came from a lack of satiety that was deep within her soul. Like us this woman looked for instant gratification to satisfy the thirst. Whereas her gratification came from sexual encounters with men that were not her husband, our instant gratification comes from, shopping, eating, alcoholism, drug use, attention seeking, constant social media posting and sexual encounters. Using anything as quick fix to calm an urge that springs up cyclically is a result of the thirst. So, we cannot judge but only identify and sympathize with the Samaritan women. One does not know why the Samaritan women chose to be promiscuous, maybe she was exposed to a perverted touch or violated as a child and now she cannot help it, or maybe she had to do what she had to do to live. Whatever the reason the Samaritan woman was used to giving of herself to a man. In John 4 Jesus is traveling to Galilee, but he needed to go through Samaria. Jesus arrives in Samaria he goes to a village named Sychar and he rests on Jacobs well it was about noon. Jesus sees the woman coming to the well to draw water, He asks her Give to me drink. Is not this coincidental, Jesus just so happening to get tired, thirsty, goes to a well and a woman who is probably tired and thirsty comes to the same well. Coincidence, I think not. This is the strategic planning of God getting his will done. The woman responded to Jesus's request for a drink as "Why are you talking to me?" It was social custom for Jews not to speak with Samaritans. Jesus was aware but did not care. Gods' inherent nature is a provider-he sent Jesus to fulfill a need that the women did not know she had. Their dialogue continues, Jesus tells her if you knew who you were speaking to you would ask me for a drink. The Samaritan woman tell Jesus, you do not have anything to draw water from the well with. But didn't she come to the well with the intentions to draw water; doesn't she have pots? The Samaritan woman probably thought Jesus is no different from any other man that wanted her to give some part of herself to him. Jesus lets her know if she drinks the living water, HE has she will never thirst again; she wants to drink of this water so that she will not have to keep coming back to this same spot time after time to try to quench the thirst. Jesus tell her she can have some but first go get her husband, she lets him know she is not married. Jesus was already aware and told her she has had five husbands and the guy you are with now is not your husband. The Samaritan woman became very humble very quick when he showed her that the longing she had was in her soul, not her body. Jesus meets her where she is, geographically and spiritually and he still communed with her. One of the names of God is El Roi "the God who sees ME". We give him praise because it matters not where you are in life God still sees you. Not the masked you, but the hurting you, you with the issue, you with the regrets, and he still wants to be with You. The Lord does not care where you are, just come and drink of the living waters. Jesus knew of her lifestyle but did not care because the need for her soul to be quenched was far more important than the cyclic behaviors she had been participating in.

There was an exchange in that conversation, she was truthful in worship, and Jesus gave her freedom. She left her water pots, went to the city, and began to spread her testimony saying" Come see a man who told me everything I ever did- Is he not the Christ?" People came to see Jesus because of her testimony and before Jesus left many believed because they saw for themselves. Even though we have the testimony of others we must experience God for ourselves, we cannot go to heaven on our family's prayers, we must see HIM for ourselves.

There is never a time when we cannot drink of the living waters of God, every believer has a well of living water on the inside of them. The way we draw and drink of this well is through worship. Reminding ourselves of Gods awesome love towards us is worship, living a life that is pleasing to him is Worship, paying tithes is Worship, giving testimony is worship. Worship is giving of ourselves to God. And through this worship we are exchanging the heaviness of carrying our burden filled proverbial waterpots for the refreshing joy of the Lord.

Chapter Objectives

- Jesus meets us at our place of need.

- No need to be ashamed of your past, God already knows.

- **WE** overcome by the words of **OUR** testimony.

- God has no respect of persons- if you want him you can access him.

- There is an exchange in worship that will leave your soul joyfully refreshed.

- Only the relationship with God satisfies the thirsty soul.

Final Words

Early Will I Seek Him for SALVATION

... I have set before thee this day life and good, and death and evil; Deuteronomy 30:15.

Everything points back to Christ. Life is about decisions. Every person discussed in this book had a choice. They could have chosen to not believe or not, Forgive or not forgive, conform to the World or not to Conform, Do Gods Will or Not. We all have Choices, and today as you have read this book, you must make a Choice. Where do you want to spend eternity? It is your choice.

Romans 10: 9-10 KJV That if thou shalt confess with thy mouth the Lord Jesus, and shalt believe in thine heart that God hath raised him from the dead, thou shalt be saved.10 For with the heart man believeth unto righteousness; and with the mouth confession is made unto salvation.

Today is the time to accept salvation. 2Cor. 6:2. **Come as You Are**!!! You do not have to know everything about the bible, find a church that can teach you. Do not allow people, or your past mistakes to stop you from becoming a Christian. He already knows about you and STILL wants to be in relationship with us. **Time is winding up Christ is Soon to Return**… Do you know Jesus as your Lord and Savior? If not, salvation is as easy as A.B.C.

Acknowledge you are a sinner,

Believe in your Heart God raised Christ from the dead,

Confess with your mouth I am saved. Romans 10:9

References

1. Understanding the Eight Prayer Watches.
   https://unitedinchristcanton.org/

   Understanding the Eight Prayer Watches.   Retrieved on December 31, 2020.

2. National Research Council (US) Committee on Disability Determination for Individuals with Hearing Impairments; Dobie RA, Van Hemel S, editors. Hearing Loss: Determining Eligibility for Social Security Benefits. Washington (DC): National Academies Press (US); 2004. 7, Hearing Loss in Children. Available from: https://www.ncbi.nlm.nih.gov/books/NBK207837/

3. Howley Elaine, K. 2019. What Mental Health Statistics Can Tell Us. Retrieved from https://health.usnews.com/conditions/mental-health/articles/what-mental-health-statistics-can-tell-us1 on 12.31.2020

4. Stein DJ, Phillips KA, Bolton D, Fulford KW, Sadler JZ, Kendler KS. What is a mental/psychiatric disorder? From DSM-IV to DSM-V. *Psychol Med.* 2010;40(11):1759–1765. doi:10.1017/S0033291709992261.

About the Author

Andrea C. Dexter is a Licensed Social Worker in the State of Mississippi, a two-time Alumna of the University of Southern Mississippi in Hattiesburg MS, and a graduate of the C.H. Mason Jurisdictional Institutes' Certification Program, Author, and owner of Reflections of the Son LLC. She worships and is a member of China Grove Church of God in Christ located in Tylertown, MS.

I encourage everyone to learn of the truth of the Lord. When there is an understanding of the truth of God it is hard to be deceived. Get to know the truth of God and experience the freedom privilege that comes with being a child of God. This understanding comes through intimate time of prayer, meditations, and reading the Word of God so that He can reveal himself to you. Get to know Him and he will tell you his secrets, you will be His friend-invest in **That** part. Do Everything to the Glory of God and HE will continue to put you in places so that you can continue to bring Him Glory.

Trends change- Favor is deceitful, and beauty is vain: but a woman that fears the Lord, she shall be praised Proverbs 31:30.

-Andrea

www.ingramcontent.com/pod-product-compliance
Lightning Source LLC
LaVergne TN
LVHW052036080426
835513LV00018B/2343